30-Minute Meals

by LORENE FROHLING

Ideals Publishing Corporation • Nashville, Tennessee 37214

Contents

Menus with Beef 5

Menus with Pork and Sausage 13

Menus with Chicken 32

Menus with Fish 45

Menus for Brunch 57

Index 64

First published as *Quick Meals*

ISBN 0-8249-3077-0
Copyright © MCMLXXXV by Ideals Publishing Corp.
All rights reserved.
Printed and bound in the United States of America.

Published by Ideals Publishing Corporation
Nelson Place at Elm Hill Pike
P.O. Box 148000
Nashville, Tennessee 37214-8000

Cover recipe:
Jambalaya, page 16.

Beef Stroganoff, page 8.

ABOUT THE BOOK

The menus in *30-Minute Meals* are planned with time, nutrition, and taste appeal in mind. Each menu can be prepared in approximately thirty minutes or less. The recipes have been developed to accommodate today's smaller family size, with most of the recipes making either four or six servings.

Recipes are given for the starred foods in each menu. Suggestions for other foods needed to balance the meal in nutrition, flavor, color, and texture are also included. These foods require little preparation, and in many cases can be purchased ready-to-serve.

To speed your shopping, an organized list of ingredients is included with each menu. Only the staple ingredients of salt and pepper are excluded.

Finally, an order of preparation tasks is suggested with each menu. This sequence is designed to organize the meal preparation and to keep the total time you spend in the kitchen to a minimum.

ABOUT THE AUTHOR

Lorene Frohling is a free-lance food writer and consultant. She holds a degree in home economics from Kansas State University. She has worked in the field of education and as an associate food editor in the development and writing of several nationally distributed cookbooks.

Menus with Beef

Skillet Barbecues*
Potato Chips
Crisp Relishes   Dill Dip*
Fresh Sliced Peaches

Shopping List:
  1 pound ground beef
  1 medium onion
  ¾ cup sour cream
  ¼ cup mayonnaise *or* salad
    dressing
  8 hamburger buns
  ½ cup catsup
  1 teaspoon prepared mustard
  1 teaspoon Worcestershire sauce
  ½ cup chili sauce
  1 tablespoon vinegar
  1 tablespoon instant minced onion
  1 teaspoon dried dillweed

  1 teaspoon dried parsley flakes
  ½ teaspoon sugar
  ¼ teaspoon celery salt
  ¼ teaspoon seasoning salt

Suggested Foods to Complete Menu:
  Potato chips
  Crisp relishes
  Fresh sliced peaches

Preparation Sequence:
  1. Prepare Dill Dip and chill.
  2. Combine ingredients for Skillet
    Barbecues and simmer.
  3. Prepare relishes and sliced peaches.

SKILLET BARBECUES

Makes 8 sandwiches

1 pound ground beef
1 medium onion, chopped
½ cup catsup
½ cup chili sauce
1 tablespoon vinegar
1 teaspoon prepared mustard
1 teaspoon Worcestershire sauce
½ teaspoon sugar
¼ teaspoon celery salt
8 hamburger buns, split

In a skillet, cook ground beef and onion until meat is brown and onion is tender; drain thoroughly. Stir in catsup, chili sauce, vinegar, mustard, Worcestershire, sugar and celery salt. Simmer, uncovered, for 15 minutes. Spoon into hamburger buns.

DILL DIP

Makes 1 cup

¾ cup sour cream
¼ cup mayonnaise *or* **salad dressing**
1 tablespoon instant minced onion
1 teaspoon dried dillweed
1 teaspoon dried parsley flakes
¼ teaspoon seasoning salt

In a bowl, combine sour cream, mayonnaise, onion, dillweed, parsley and salt; cover and chill. Serve with crisp relishes.

Beef with Peppers and Tomatoes*
Hot Cooked Rice
Boston Lettuce Salad*
Fresh Pineapple

Shopping List:
  1 pound beef tenderloin or sirloin
    steak
  1 large green pepper
  1 cup halved cherry tomatoes
  2 small heads Boston lettuce
  1 teaspoon snipped parsley
  1 ounce shredded Cheddar cheese
  ½ cup sour cream
  2 tablespoons cooking oil
    Rice
  ¼ cup Italian salad dressing
  2 tablespoons mayonnaise or salad
    dressing
  2 tablespoons soy sauce
  2 tablespoons dry sherry
  1 teaspoon cornstarch
  ½ teaspoon sugar

Suggested Foods to Complete Menu:
  Fresh pineapple

Preparation Sequence:
  1. Cook rice according to package
     directions.
  2. Combine dressing ingredients for
     Boston Lettuce Salad.
  3. Prepare pineapple.
  4. Prepare Beef with Peppers and
     Tomatoes.
  5. Arrange salads on salad plates.

BEEF WITH PEPPERS AND TOMATOES

Makes 4 servings

1 pound beef tenderloin or **sirloin steak**
1 teaspoon cornstarch
½ teaspoon sugar
¼ teaspoon salt
2 tablespoons dry sherry
2 tablespoons soy sauce
2 tablespoons cooking oil
1 large green pepper, cut into strips
1 cup halved cherry tomatoes
  Hot cooked rice

Slice beef thinly across the grain into bite-sized strips. In a small bowl, combine cornstarch, sugar and salt. Stir in sherry and soy sauce; set aside. Preheat a wok or large skillet over high heat; add oil. Stir-fry beef and green pepper in hot oil for 3 to 4 minutes or until meat is brown and pepper is tender-crisp. Stir cornstarch mixture; blend into meat mixture. Cook and stir until thick and bubbly. Stir in tomatoes. Cook and stir until heated through. Serve with rice.

BOSTON LETTUCE SALAD

Makes 4 servings

½ cup sour cream
¼ cup Italian salad dressing
2 tablespoons mayonnaise or **salad dressing**
1 teaspoon snipped parsley
2 small heads Boston lettuce
¼ cup shredded Cheddar cheese

To make dressing, in a screw-top jar, combine sour cream, salad dressing, mayonnaise and parsley. Core lettuce; cut each head in half. Arrange lettuce on salad plates; top with dressing. Sprinkle with cheese.

Taco Salad, page 12.

Beef Stroganoff*
Hot Cooked Noodles
Asparagus with Sesame Seed*
Tomato-Cucumber Salad*
Apple-Blueberry Crisp*

Shopping List:
1 pound beef tenderloin *or* sirloin steak
1½ pounds fresh asparagus
3 medium tomatoes
1 medium cucumber
2 cups sliced fresh mushrooms
½ cup chopped onion
   Lettuce leaves
1 cup fresh *or* frozen blueberries
1 tablespoon lemon juice
1 cup sour cream
½ cup butter *or* margarine
   Vanilla ice cream, optional
⅓ cup salad oil
   Noodles
1 can (21 ounces) apple pie filling
¼ cup quick-cooking rolled oats
6 tablespoons flour
¼ cup brown sugar
1 tablespoon granulated sugar
3 tablespoons white wine vinegar

2 teaspoons Worcestershire sauce
1 tablespoon sesame seed
1 teaspoon instant beef bouillon
   granules
½ teaspoon cinnamon
½ teaspoon dried basil
¼ teaspoon celery salt
   Paprika

Preparation Sequence:
1. Marinate tomatoes and cucumber in dressing mixture.
2. Prepare Apple-Blueberry Crisp.
3. Clean asparagus.
4. Brown meat in butter or margarine.
5. Cook asparagus.
6. Cook noodles according to package directions.
7. Complete preparation of Beef Stroganoff.
8. Arrange salads on salad plates.

BEEF STROGANOFF

Makes 6 servings

1 pound beef tenderloin *or* **sirloin steak**
2 tablespoons butter *or* **margarine**
2 cups sliced fresh mushrooms
½ cup chopped onion
½ cup water
2 teaspoons Worcestershire sauce
1 teaspoon instant beef bouillon granules
½ teaspoon salt
1 cup sour cream
2 tablespoons flour
   Hot cooked noodles
   Paprika

Slice beef thinly across the grain into bite-sized strips. In a medium skillet, brown meat in hot butter over medium-high heat, stirring occasionally. Add mushrooms and onion; sauté for 3 to 4 minutes or until onion is tender-crisp. Stir in water, Worcestershire, bouillon granules and salt; bring to a boil. In a small bowl, stir together sour cream and flour; stir into meat mixture. Cook and stir over medium heat until thick and bubbly; cook and stir for 1 minute more. Serve over hot noodles; sprinkle with paprika.

ASPARAGUS WITH SESAME SEED

Makes 6 servings

½ **cup water**
½ **teaspoon salt**
1½ **pounds fresh asparagus, cut into**
  1½-inch lengths
2 **tablespoons butter** *or* **margarine**
1 **tablespoon sesame seed, toasted**
2 **teaspoons lemon juice**

In a saucepan, bring water and salt to a boil; add asparagus. Cook, covered, about 8 minutes or until tender. Drain. Stir in butter, sesame seed and lemon juice.

TOMATO-CUCUMBER SALAD

Makes 6 servings

3 **medium tomatoes, thinly sliced**
1 **medium cucumber, thinly sliced**
⅓ **cup salad oil**
3 **tablespoons white wine vinegar**
1 **tablespoon sugar**
½ **teaspoon crushed dried basil**
¼ **teaspoon celery salt**
  Lettuce leaves

Place tomatoes and cucumber in a shallow dish. To make dressing, in a screw-top jar, combine oil, vinegar, sugar, basil and celery salt; shake and pour over tomatoes and cucumber. Cover and chill until serving time. To serve, place lettuce on 6 individual salad plates. Arrange tomatoes and cucumber atop lettuce.

APPLE-BLUEBERRY CRISP

Makes 6 servings

1 **can (21 ounces) apple pie filling**
1 **cup fresh** *or* **frozen blueberries**
1 **teaspoon lemon juice**
¼ **cup quick-cooking rolled oats**
¼ **cup flour**
¼ **cup brown sugar**
½ **teaspoon cinnamon**
¼ **cup butter** *or* **margarine**
  Vanilla ice cream, optional

Combine pie filling, blueberries and lemon juice; turn into a 9-inch pie plate. In a bowl, combine oats, flour, brown sugar and cinnamon; cut in butter until mixture resembles coarse crumbs. Sprinkle over fruit. Bake at 350° for 25 to 30 minutes or until bubbly. Serve warm with vanilla ice cream, if desired.

Steak and Onions*
Hash Browns with Cheese*
Fresh Green Salad
Cantaloupe A La Mode

Shopping List:
4 beef cube steaks, about 1 pound each
1 large onion
1 package (12 ounces) frozen loose-pack hash brown potatoes
1 cup shredded Swiss *or* Cheddar cheese
2 tablespoons butter *or* margarine
5 tablespoons cooking oil
½ cup dry red *or* white wine
¼ cup soy sauce
Garlic powder

Suggested Foods to Complete Menu:
Green salad
Cantaloupe
Vanilla ice cream

Preparation Sequence:
1. Marinate cube steaks for Steak and Onions.
2. Prepare a green salad.
3. Cut cantaloupe.
4. Cook onion in butter.
5. Start cooking Hash Browns with Cheese.
6. Cook marinated steaks.

STEAK AND ONIONS

Makes 4 servings

½ **cup dry red** *or* **white wine**
¼ **cup soy sauce**
Dash garlic powder
4 **beef cube steaks, about 1 pound each**
1 **large onion, sliced and separated into rings**
2 **tablespoons butter** *or* **margarine**
1 **tablespoon cooking oil**

In a large shallow baking dish, combine wine, soy sauce and garlic powder. Arrange steaks in a single layer in the baking dish; cover and marinate at room temperature, about 45 minutes. (Or, marinate in the refrigerator for 4 to 6 hours.) In a large skillet, cook and stir onion in hot butter over medium-high heat for 4 to 5 minutes or until tender. Remove from skillet; keep warm. Drain steaks. In the same skillet, cook steaks in hot oil over medium-high heat for 3 minutes; turn and cook for 2 to 3 minutes more or until done. Serve with onions.

HASH BROWNS WITH CHEESE

Makes 4 servings

¼ **cup cooking oil**
1 **package (12 ounces) frozen loose-pack hash brown potatoes**
½ **teaspoon salt**
1 **cup shredded Swiss** *or* **Cheddar cheese**

In a large skillet, heat oil over medium-high heat. Add potatoes; spread into an even layer. Sprinkle with salt. Cover and cook over medium-high heat for 6 minutes; stir. Cover and cook for 3 to 4 minutes more or until golden brown. Remove from heat. Add cheese and toss; cover for 1 minute.

Beef with Peppers and Tomatoes, page 6.

Taco Salad*
Tortilla Chips
Banana Peppers
Vanilla Ice Cream
Hot Butter-Pecan Sauce*

Shopping List:
1 pound ground beef
1 small onion
4 cups shredded lettuce
2 medium tomatoes
½ cup sour cream
¾ cup shredded Cheddar cheese
¼ cup butter or margarine
  Vanilla ice cream
  Tortilla chips
½ cup taco sauce
  Pitted ripe olives
¼ cup finely chopped pecans
½ cup sugar
½ teaspoon vanilla

Suggested Foods to Complete Menu:
Banana peppers

Preparation Sequence:
1. Prepare ground beef for Taco Salad and chill.
2. Prepare Hot Butter-Pecan Sauce.
3. Assemble salads on individual salad plates.

TACO SALAD

Makes 4 servings

1 pound ground beef
1 small onion, chopped
½ cup taco sauce
½ cup sour cream
¼ teaspoon salt
4 cups shredded lettuce
¾ cup shredded Cheddar cheese
2 medium tomatoes, chopped
  Sliced pitted ripe olives
  Tortilla chips

In a medium skillet, cook and stir ground beef and onion over medium-high heat until meat is brown and onion is tender. Drain thoroughly. In a bowl, combine meat mixture, taco sauce, half of the sour cream and salt. Cover and chill for 20 to 30 minutes. To serve, place lettuce on 4 individual salad plates. Sprinkle with cheese and tomatoes. Spoon meat mixture over salads. Top with remaining sour cream and garnish with olive slices. Serve with tortilla chips.

HOT BUTTER-PECAN SAUCE

Makes about ½ cup

¼ cup finely chopped pecans
¼ cup butter *or* margarine
½ cup sugar
¼ cup water
½ teaspoon vanilla
  Vanilla ice cream

In a small saucepan, cook pecans in butter over medium heat until golden. Stir in sugar and water. Bring to a boil. Reduce heat and simmer, uncovered, about 5 minutes or until slightly thickened, stirring often. Remove from heat; stir in vanilla. Serve warm over ice cream.

Menus with Pork and Sausage

Barbecue-Style Pork Chops*
Hash Browns Au Gratin*
Mixed Vegetable Salad*
Melon in Citrus Sauce*

Shopping List:

4 pork chops, about 1 pound
1 package (12 ounces) frozen loose-pack hash brown potatoes
1 box (10 ounces) frozen mixed vegetables
4 onion slices
½ cup halved cherry tomatoes
Lettuce leaves
2 cups cubed honeydew melon
2 cups cubed cantaloupe
4 lemon slices
¼ cup orange juice
3 tablespoons lime juice
1 cup whipping cream
¼ cup shredded American cheese
½ cup tomato juice
¼ cup catsup
½ cup Green Goddess salad dressing
2 tablespoons sliced pitted ripe olives
¼ cup granulated sugar
1 tablespoon brown sugar
1 tablespoon vinegar
1 teaspoon Worcestershire sauce
¼ teaspoon chili powder

Preparation Sequence:

1. Cook frozen mixed vegetables.
2. Bake pork chops with lemon and onion slices.
3. Combine ingredients for Hash Browns Au Gratin.
4. Prepare barbecue sauce, then pour over chops.
5. Place chops and potatoes in the oven.
6. Combine mixed vegetables with salad dressing and chill.
7. Prepare Melon in Citrus Sauce.
8. Complete preparation of Mixed Vegetable Salad.

BARBECUE-STYLE PORK CHOPS

Makes 4 servings

4 pork chops (about 1 pound)
4 lemon slices
4 onion slices
½ cup tomato juice
¼ cup catsup
1 tablespoon brown sugar
1 tablespoon vinegar
1 teaspoon Worcestershire sauce
¼ teaspoon chili powder

Arrange chops in a single layer in a shallow baking dish. Cover chops with lemon and onion slices. Bake, uncovered, at 450° for 10 minutes. In a small saucepan, combine tomato juice, catsup, brown sugar, vinegar, Worcestershire and chili powder. Bring to a boil. Drain chops; pour sauce over all. Reduce oven temperature to 375°. Continue baking chops, uncovered, for 40 to 45 minutes or until tender. Baste occasionally with sauce.

HASH BROWNS AU GRATIN

Makes 4 servings

1 **package (12 ounces) frozen loose-pack hash brown potatoes**
1 **cup whipping cream**
½ **teaspoon salt**
¼ **cup shredded American cheese**

Arrange frozen potatoes in a 1-quart casserole. Pour whipping cream over all; sprinkle with salt. Bake, uncovered, at 375° about 45 minutes or until potatoes are tender and saucy, stirring once or twice. Sprinkle with cheese the last 5 minutes.

MIXED VEGETABLE SALAD

Makes 4 servings

1 **box (10 ounces) frozen mixed vegetables**
½ **cup Green Goddess salad dressing**
½ **cup halved cherry tomatoes**
2 **tablespoons sliced pitted ripe olives**
    Lettuce leaves

Cook vegetables; rinse under cold water and drain thoroughly. Pour dressing over vegetables; cover and chill at least 30 minutes. Stir in tomatoes and ripe olives. Serve on lettuce leaves.

MELON IN CITRUS SAUCE

Makes 4 servings

¼ **cup sugar**
¼ **cup orange juice**
3 **tablespoons lime juice**
2 **cups cubed honeydew melon**
2 **cups cubed cantaloupe**

In a bowl, combine sugar, orange juice and lime juice; stir until sugar dissolves. Add honeydew and cantaloupe; stir gently. Cover and chill. Stir again before serving.

Fresh Fruit with Marmalade Cream, page 25.

*Jambalaya**
*Fresh Greens   Honey-French Dressing**
*Parmesan-Parsley Rolls**
*Chocolate Cake with Broiled Icing**

Shopping List:
  1 cup cubed fully cooked ham
  1 cup cooked shrimp
  1 medium green pepper
  2 green onions
  1 onion slice
  1 tablespoon snipped parsley
  ½ cup butter or margarine
  2 tablespoons whipping cream
  2 tablespoons grated Parmesan cheese
  ⅓ cup salad oil
  ¾ cup long-grain rice
  1 package refrigerated crescent rolls
  1 frozen unfrosted chocolate cake (1 layer)
  1 can (28 ounces) tomatoes
  ⅓ cup vinegar
  ⅓ cup catsup
  ⅓ cup honey
  ¼ cup brown sugar
  ½ teaspoon sugar
  ¼ cup chopped nuts
  1 teaspoon instant beef bouillon granules
  1 bay leaf
  ½ teaspoon celery seed
  ¼ teaspoon dry mustard
  Hot pepper sauce

Suggested Foods to Complete Menu:
  Fresh greens

Preparation Sequence:
  1. Prepare Honey-French Dressing and chill.
  2. Combine icing ingredients and spread over frozen cake.
  3. Start Jambalaya and let simmer until rice is tender.
  4. Prepare Parmesan-Parsley Rolls and bake.
  5. Stir shrimp and green pepper into Jambalaya.
  6. Toss fresh greens with dressing.

JAMBALAYA

Makes 4 or 5 servings

1 cup cubed fully cooked ham
2 green onions, chopped
1 tablespoon butter or **margarine**
1 can (28 ounces) tomatoes, undrained
1 cup water
¾ cup long-grain rice
1 bay leaf
1 teaspoon instant beef bouillon granules
½ teaspoon sugar
  Dash hot pepper sauce
1 cup cooked shrimp, halved
1 medium green pepper, cut into 1-inch squares

In a large saucepan, cook and stir ham and green onions in hot butter over medium-high heat for 3 to 4 minutes or until onions are tender. Stir in tomatoes, water, rice, bay leaf, bouillon granules, sugar and hot pepper sauce. Bring to a boil. Reduce heat and simmer, covered, about 15 minutes or until rice is tender. Stir in shrimp and green pepper. Simmer, uncovered, for 6 to 8 minutes or until of desired consistency. Remove bay leaf before serving.

HONEY-FRENCH DRESSING

Makes 1 cup

⅓ **cup vinegar**
⅓ **cup catsup**
⅓ **cup honey**
 1 **onion slice**
½ **teaspoon celery seed**
¼ **teaspoon dry mustard**
⅓ **cup salad oil**
   Fresh greens

In a blender container, combine vinegar, catsup, honey, onion, celery seed and dry mustard; cover and blend until smooth. With blender running, gradually add oil. Cover and chill. Serve with fresh greens.

PARMESAN-PARSLEY ROLLS

Makes 8 rolls

¼ **cup butter** or **margarine, softened**
 2 **tablespoons grated Parmesan cheese**
 1 **tablespoon snipped parsley**
 1 **package refrigerated crescent rolls**

Combine butter, Parmesan and parsley. Unroll crescent dough and separate into 8 triangles. Spread triangles with butter mixture. Roll up and bake.

CHOCOLATE CAKE WITH BROILED ICING

Makes 4 or 5 servings

 1 **frozen unfrosted chocolate cake**
   (1 layer)
¼ **cup brown sugar**
¼ **cup chopped nuts**
 3 **tablespoons butter** or **margarine,**
   softened
 2 **tablespoons whipping cream**

Place frozen cake on a baking sheet. Combine brown sugar, nuts, butter and whipping cream; spread over frozen cake. Let stand for 30 minutes. Just before serving, preheat broiler. Broil cake 4 inches from heat about 1 minute or until frosting is bubbly. Serve immediately.

Broiled Ham with Apricot Glaze*
Cauliflower with Almond-Dill Butter*
Avocado-Orange Salad*
Stirred Rice Pudding*

Shopping List:
- 1 1-pound fully cooked center-cut ham slice
- 1 package (10 ounces) frozen cauliflower
- 1 avocado
- 1 small onion
  Bibb lettuce
- 2 oranges
- 1 tablespoon orange or pineapple juice
- 2 eggs
- 1 cup milk
- 2 tablespoons butter or margarine
- 1 cup cooked rice
- ½ cup clear French salad dressing
- ¼ cup raisins
- 2 tablespoons slivered almonds
- 2 tablespoons apricot preserves
- ¼ cup sugar
- 1 teaspoon vanilla
- ½ teaspoon Dijon-style mustard
- ¼ teaspoon dried dillweed
  Cinnamon

Preparation Sequence:
1. Prepare Stirred Rice Pudding and chill.
2. Arrange oranges, avocado and onion on salad plates, then chill.
3. Cook cauliflower and prepare Almond-Dill Butter.
4. Broil ham and prepare glaze.
5. Drizzle salad dressing over salads.

BROILED HAM WITH APRICOT GLAZE

Makes 4 servings

1 1-pound fully cooked center-cut ham slice
2 tablespoons apricot preserves
1 tablespoon orange or pineapple juice
½ teaspoon Dijon-style mustard

Preheat broiler. Slash fat along edge of ham slice. Place ham on an unheated rack of a broiler pan. Broil 3 inches from heat for 3 minutes. Turn and broil for 3 minutes more. In a small bowl, combine apricot preserves, orange juice and mustard; spoon over ham. Broil for ½ to 1 minute more or until glaze is bubbly.

Spaghetti Carbonara, page 27.

CAULIFLOWER WITH ALMOND-DILL BUTTER

Makes 4 servings

1 package (10 ounces) frozen cauliflower
2 tablespoons slivered almonds
2 tablespoons butter *or* margarine
¼ teaspoon dried dillweed

Cook cauliflower; drain. In a small saucepan, cook almonds in butter over low heat until golden, stirring frequently. Stir in dill. Pour over cauliflower and toss.

AVOCADO-ORANGE SALAD

Makes 4 servings

Bibb lettuce
2 oranges, peeled and sliced
1 avocado, seeded, peeled and sliced
1 small onion, sliced and separated into rings
½ cup clear French salad dressing

Line 4 salad plates with lettuce; arrange oranges, avocado and onion atop lettuce. Drizzle with salad dressing.

STIRRED RICE PUDDING

Makes 4 servings

2 eggs, beaten
1 cup milk
¼ cup sugar
¼ cup raisins
1 cup cooked rice
1 teaspoon vanilla
Dash salt
Dash cinnamon

In a saucepan, combine eggs, milk, sugar and raisins. Cook and stir over medium heat for 6 to 8 minutes or until mixture coats a metal spoon. Remove from heat; stir in rice, vanilla, salt and cinnamon. Spoon into dessert dishes. Chill until serving time.

*Minestrone with Sausage**
*Green Salad Toss**
*Italian Toast Slices**
*Cherry-Oatmeal Cobbler**

Shopping List:
  8 ounces bulk Italian sausage
  1 small onion
  1 carrot
  1 small zucchini
  4 cups torn lettuce
  2 cups torn curly endive
  ½ medium green pepper
  2 cups cauliflower florets
  1 package (16 ounces) frozen
    unsweetened pitted tart red cherries
  ¼ cup grated Parmesan cheese
  9 tablespoons butter *or* margarine
  ⅓ cup olive *or* salad oil
  12 slices Italian bread
  ¾ cup small shell macaroni
  1 can (16 ounces) tomatoes
  1 can (15 ounces) Great Northern beans
  ⅓ roll refrigerated oatmeal cookie
    dough

  ¾ cup sugar
  1 tablespoon cornstarch
  3 tablespoons vinegar
  2 teaspoons instant beef bouillon
    granules
  1 teaspoon dried oregano
  ½ teaspoon dried basil
  ¼ teaspoon almond extract
    Garlic powder

Preparation Sequence:
  1. Start preparation of Minestrone with
     Sausage.
  2. Prepare Cherry-Oatmeal Cobbler.
  3. Spread Italian bread with butter
     mixture.
  4. Combine salad ingredients for Green
     Salad Toss.
  5. Broil Italian Toast Slices.
  6. Toss salad with dressing.

MINESTRONE WITH SAUSAGE

Makes 6 servings

8 ounces bulk Italian sausage
1 small onion, chopped
1 carrot, chopped
2 cups water
1 can (16 ounces) tomatoes, undrained
**1 can (15 ounces) Great Northern beans,
  drained**
**2 teaspoons instant beef bouillon
  granules**
1 teaspoon salt
**½ teaspoon crushed dried basil
  Dash garlic powder**
¾ cup small shell macaroni
**1 small zucchini, chopped
  Grated Parmesan cheese**

In a Dutch oven, cook sausage, onion and carrot over medium-high heat until meat is brown and vegetables are tender, stirring occasionally; drain. Add water, tomatoes, beans, bouillon granules, salt, basil and garlic powder. Bring to a boil. Reduce heat and simmer, covered, for 20 minutes. Stir in macaroni; simmer, covered, for 5 minutes. Stir in zucchini; simmer, uncovered, about 5 minutes or until zucchini and macaroni are tender, stirring occasionally. Serve with Parmesan.

GREEN SALAD TOSS

Makes 6 servings

4 cups torn lettuce
2 cups torn curly endive
½ medium green pepper, sliced
2 cups cauliflower florets
⅓ cup olive *or* salad oil
3 tablespoons vinegar
  Dash garlic powder
  Dash salt
  Freshly ground black pepper

In a salad bowl, combine lettuce, endive, green pepper and cauliflower. For dressing, in a screw-top jar, combine oil, vinegar, garlic powder, salt and pepper; shake thoroughly. Pour dressing over salad; toss lightly.

ITALIAN TOAST SLICES

Makes 12 slices

½ cup butter *or* margarine, softened
¼ cup grated Parmesan cheese
1 teaspoon crushed dried oregano
12 slices Italian bread

Preheat broiler. Combine butter, Parmesan and oregano; spread on one side of each bread slice. Place bread, buttered-side-up, on a baking sheet. Broil 2 to 3 inches from heat for 1 to 2 minutes or until toasted.

CHERRY-OATMEAL COBBLER

Makes 6 servings

1 package (16 ounces) frozen
  unsweetened pitted tart red cherries,
  thawed
¾ cup sugar
1 tablespoon cornstarch
1 tablespoon butter *or* margarine
¼ teaspoon almond extract
⅓ roll refrigerated oatmeal cookie
  dough

Drain cherries, reserving juice; set cherries aside. If needed, add water to juice to make ½ cup. In a saucepan, combine sugar and cornstarch; stir in juice. Cook and stir over medium heat until thick and bubbly; stir in reserved cherries, butter and almond extract. Heat and stir until bubbly. Cut cookie dough into 6 slices. Turn hot cherry mixture into a 1½-quart casserole. Top with cookie dough slices. Bake at 400° for about 20 minutes or until bubbly.

Barbecue-Style Pork Chops, page 13.

Mostaccioli Bake*
Seasoned Italian Green Beans*
Garlic Bread*
Fresh Fruit with Marmalade Cream*

Shopping List:
  8 ounces bulk Italian sausage
  1 package (9 ounces) frozen Italian
    green beans
  1 tablespoon snipped parsley
  3 cups mixed fresh fruit
  ½ cup cream-style cottage cheese
  ½ cup plus ⅓ cup sour cream
  1 cup shredded Mozzarella cheese
  ¼ cup butter or margarine
  6 ounces mostaccioli
  8 slices Italian bread
  1 cup meatless spaghetti sauce
  2 tablespoons regular onion soup mix
  1 tablespoon chopped pimiento

  1 tablespoon orange marmalade
  ¼ teaspoon dried oregano
  ¼ teaspoon garlic powder
    Paprika
    Nutmeg

Preparation Sequence:
  1. Prepare Mostaccioli Bake.
  2. Spread bread with garlic butter and
     wrap in foil.
  3. Combine ingredients for Marmalade
     Cream.
  4. Prepare Seasoned Italian Green
     Beans.
  5. Heat bread.
  6. Prepare fresh fruit.

MOSTACCIOLI BAKE

Makes 4 servings

8 ounces bulk Italian sausage
1 cup meatless spaghetti sauce
½ cup cream-style cottage cheese
½ cup sour cream
1 cup shredded Mozzarella cheese
1 tablespoon snipped parsley
**6 ounces mostaccioli, cooked and
    drained**

In a skillet, brown sausage; drain. Stir in spaghetti sauce; set aside. In a bowl, combine cottage cheese, sour cream, ½ cup of Mozzarella and parsley. In a 10 x 6 x 2-inch baking dish, layer mostaccioli; spread cheese mixture over pasta. Spoon meat mixture over all. Sprinkle with remaining Mozzarella. Bake, uncovered, at 375° for 30 to 35 minutes or until heated through.

SEASONED ITALIAN GREEN BEANS

Makes 4 servings

1 package (9 ounces) frozen Italian
   green beans, cooked
2 tablespoons regular onion soup mix
¼ teaspoon crushed dried oregano
1 tablespoon chopped pimiento

Cook beans adding dry onion soup mix and oregano to water. Drain and stir in pimiento.

GARLIC BREAD

Makes 8 slices

¼ cup butter *or* margarine, softened
¼ teaspoon garlic powder
   Dash paprika
8 slices Italian bread

Combine butter, garlic powder and paprika. Spread on 1 side of each bread slice. Stack slices with buttered sides together; wrap in foil. Heat at 375°, about 15 minutes or until hot.

FRESH FRUIT WITH MARMALADE CREAM

Makes 4 servings

⅓ cup sour cream
1 tablespoon orange marmalade
   Dash nutmeg
3 cups mixed fresh fruit (sliced
   strawberries, sliced bananas,
   blueberries, *or* pineapple chunks)

Combine sour cream, marmalade and nutmeg. Spoon fruit into dessert dishes; top with sour cream mixture.

*Spaghetti Carbonara**
*Italian Salad**
*Seasoned Bread Sticks**
*Chocolate-Marshmallow Pudding**

Shopping List:
½ pound bacon
4 cups torn romaine
2 tablespoons snipped parsley
3 eggs
⅔ cup plus ¼ cup grated Parmesan cheese
¾ cup light cream
¼ cup milk
¼ cup butter *or* margarine
½ cup olive *or* salad oil
1 tablespoon mayonnaise *or* salad dressing
1 container (4 ounces) frozen whipped dessert topping
12 ounces spaghetti
1 package refrigerated bread sticks (8)

¼ cup seasoned croutons
10 marshmallows
1 bar (3¾ ounces) milk chocolate
¼ cup tarragon vinegar
1 teaspoon Dijon-style mustard
¾ teaspoon dried oregano
¼ teaspoon dried basil
Nutmeg
Garlic powder

Preparation Sequence:
1. Prepare Chocolate-Marshmallow Pudding and chill.
2. Prepare dressing for Italian Salad.
3. Combine ingredients for Seasoned Bread Sticks and bake.
4. Prepare Spaghetti Carbonara.
5. Toss salad with dressing.

SPAGHETTI CARBONARA

Makes 4 servings

3 eggs
¾ cup light cream
½ pound bacon, cut up
12 ounces spaghetti
2 tablespoons butter *or* **margarine**
⅔ cup grated Parmesan cheese
2 tablespoons snipped parsley
Dash nutmeg

Beat eggs; blend in cream. Set aside. In a skillet, fry bacon until crisp; drain. Set aside. Cook spaghetti and drain; toss with butter until melted. Pour egg mixture over spaghetti; add bacon, Parmesan, parsley and nutmeg. Toss until well coated. Serve immediately.

ITALIAN SALAD

Makes 4 servings

¼ **cup tarragon vinegar**
1 **tablespoon mayonnaise** *or* **salad dressing**
1 **teaspoon Dijon-style mustard**
½ **teaspoon crushed dried oregano**
 Dash garlic powder
½ **cup olive** *or* **salad oil**
4 **cups torn romaine**
¼ **cup grated Parmesan cheese**
¼ **cup seasoned croutons**

To make dressing, in a screw-top jar, combine vinegar, mayonnaise, mustard, oregano and garlic powder. Using a whisk, slowly blend in oil, beating constantly. In a salad bowl, combine romaine, Parmesan and croutons; pour dressing over all and toss.

SEASONED BREAD STICKS

Makes 8 sticks

2 **tablespoons butter** *or* **margarine, melted**
¼ **teaspoon crushed dried basil**
¼ **teaspoon crushed dried oregano**
1 **package refrigerated bread sticks**

Combine butter, basil and oregano. Prepare bread sticks for baking; brush with butter mixture. Bake at 350° for 15 to 18 minutes or until lightly browned.

CHOCOLATE-MARSHMALLOW PUDDING

Makes 4 servings

10 **marshmallows**
¼ **cup milk**
1 **bar (3¾ ounces) milk chocolate**
1 **container (4 ounces) frozen whipped dessert topping, thawed**

In the top of a double boiler, heat marshmallows and milk over hot water until melted; add chocolate and stir until melted and smooth. Transfer to a metal bowl; chill in the refrigerator, about 15 minutes or until cooled, stirring occasionally. Fold in whipped topping. Spoon into dessert dishes. Place in the freezer until serving time.

Pork Chops with Brown Rice*
Broiled Tomatoes*
Mixed Green Salad*   Blue Cheese Dressing*
Apple Pie

Shopping List:
4 pork chops, about 1 pound
1 stalk celery
2 large ripe tomatoes
2 cups torn leaf lettuce
2 cups torn romaine lettuce
1 cup broccoli florets
1 small zucchini
4 radishes
2 green onions
1 package (4⅝ ounces) quick-cooking brown and wild rice mix with mushrooms
¾ cup soft bread crumbs
1¼ cups sour cream
¼ cup buttermilk
¼ cup grated Parmesan cheese
¼ cup crumbled blue cheese

2 tablespoons butter or margarine
1 tablespoon cooking oil
1 tablespoon vinegar
1 teaspoon sugar
½ teaspoon Worcestershire sauce
¼ teaspoon dried basil
   Garlic powder

Suggested Foods to Complete Menu:
Apple pie

Preparation Sequence:
1. Start preparation of Pork Chops with Brown Rice.
2. Prepare Blue Cheese Dressing.
3. Combine ingredients for Mixed Green Salad.
4. Prepare Broiled Tomatoes.
5. Toss dressing with salad.

PORK CHOPS WITH BROWN RICE

Makes 4 servings

4 pork chops, about 1 pound
1 tablespoon cooking oil
1 package (4⅝ ounces) quick-cooking brown and wild rice mix with mushrooms
1⅓ cups water
1 stalk celery, sliced
½ cup sour cream

In a skillet, brown chops in hot oil over medium heat. Remove chops from the skillet; discard drippings. In the same skillet, combine rice mix, water and celery; place chops over rice mixture. Bring to a boil. Reduce heat and simmer, covered, for 30 minutes. Remove chops from the skillet; keep warm. Stir sour cream into rice mixture; heat through, but do not boil. Serve with chops.

BROILED TOMATOES

Makes 4 servings

2 large ripe tomatoes
¾ cup soft bread crumbs
¼ cup grated Parmesan cheese
2 tablespoons butter *or* margarine, melted
¼ teaspoon dried basil, crushed

Preheat broiler. Halve each tomato cross-wise. Place, cut-side-up, in a shallow baking pan. Combine bread crumbs, Parmesan, butter and basil; sprinkle over tomatoes. Broil 3 to 4 inches from the heat about 4 minutes or until lightly browned.

MIXED GREEN SALAD

Makes 4 servings

2 cups torn leaf lettuce
2 cups torn romaine lettuce
1 cup broccoli florets
1 small zucchini, thinly sliced
4 radishes, sliced
2 green onions, sliced
   Blue Cheese Dressing

In a salad bowl, combine lettuce, romaine, broccoli, zucchini, radishes and green onion. Just before serving, toss with some of the Blue Cheese Dressing.

BLUE CHEESE DRESSING

Makes about 1 cup

¾ cup sour cream
¼ cup buttermilk
1 tablespoon vinegar
1 teaspoon sugar
½ teaspoon Worcestershire sauce
   Dash garlic powder
¼ cup crumbled blue cheese

In a bowl, combine sour cream, buttermilk, vinegar, sugar, Worcestershire and garlic powder; mix well. Stir in blue cheese. Cover and chill.

Mixed Fruit with Sherbet, page 40.

Menus with Chicken

Butter-Broiled Chicken*
Corn with Mushrooms*
Romaine and Artichoke Toss*
Raspberry or Lemon Sherbet   Blueberry Sauce*

Shopping List:

8 to 10 chicken legs or thighs
1 package (10 ounces) frozen whole
  kernel corn
3 cups torn romaine
1 cup sliced fresh mushrooms
1 tablespoon snipped parsley
1 cup fresh or frozen blueberries
1 teaspoon lemon juice
½ cup butter or margarine
¼ cup mayonnaise or salad
  dressing
1 jar (6 ounces) marinated artichoke
  hearts
3 tablespoons sugar
2 teaspoons cornstarch
2 tablespoons tarragon vinegar
1 tablespoon anchovy paste

1 teaspoon Dijon-style mustard
¼ teaspoon seasoning salt
¼ teaspoon dried oregano
  Garlic powder
  Paprika

Suggested Foods to Complete Menu:

Raspberry or lemon sherbet

Preparation Sequence:

1. Prepare Blueberry Sauce and cool.
2. Preheat broiler and combine butter sauce for chicken.
3. Begin broiling chicken.
4. Prepare dressing for salad.
5. Combine salad ingredients.
6. Turn chicken.
7. Prepare Corn with Mushrooms.
8. Toss salad with dressing.

BUTTER-BROILED CHICKEN

Makes 4 servings

6 tablespoons butter or **margarine, melted**
¼ teaspoon seasoning salt
¼ teaspoon dried oregano, crushed
  Dash garlic powder
  Dash paprika
8 to 10 chicken legs or **thighs**

Preheat broiler. Combine butter, seasoning salt, oregano, garlic powder and paprika. Place chicken, skin-side-down, on an unheated rack of a broiler pan. Brush lightly with butter mixture. Broil 5 to 6 inches from heat for 20 minutes, brushing occasionally with butter mixture. Turn; broil for 10 minutes more or until chicken is tender, brushing occasionally.

CORN WITH MUSHROOMS

Makes 4 servings

1 package (10 ounces) frozen whole kernel corn
1 cup sliced fresh mushrooms
2 tablespoons butter *or* margarine
1 tablespoon snipped parsley

Cook and drain corn. In a skillet, cook and stir mushrooms in hot butter over medium-high heat for 3 to 4 minutes or until tender. Stir in corn and parsley.

ROMAINE AND ARTICHOKE TOSS

Makes 4 servings

1 jar (6 ounces) marinated artichoke hearts
¼ cup mayonnaise *or* salad dressing
2 tablespoons tarragon vinegar
1 tablespoon anchovy paste
1 teaspoon Dijon-style mustard
3 cups torn romaine

Drain artichokes, reserving 2 tablespoons of the marinade. Cut up artichokes; set aside. To make dressing, combine mayonnaise, vinegar, anchovy paste, mustard and reserved marinade. In a bowl, combine romaine and artichokes; add dressing and toss.

BLUEBERRY SAUCE

Makes 1 cup

1 cup fresh *or* frozen blueberries, thawed
3 tablespoons sugar
2 teaspoons cornstarch
½ cup water
1 teaspoon lemon juice

In a saucepan, crush ⅓ cup of the blueberries. Combine sugar and cornstarch; stir in water. Add sugar mixture to saucepan. Cook and stir over medium heat until thick and bubbly. Cook and stir 2 minutes more. Remove from heat; stir in remaining ⅔ cup blueberries and lemon juice. Cool. Serve over sherbet.

Chicken Salad in Croissants*
Swiss Cheese Soup*
Carrot Sticks
Apple Wedges

Shopping List:
 2 cups diced cooked chicken
 1 stalk celery
   Leaf lettuce
 1 teaspoon snipped chives
3½ cups milk
 6 slices processed Swiss cheese
 3 tablespoons butter *or* margarine
 ½ cup mayonnaise *or* salad
   dressing
 4 croissants
 1 can (8¼ ounces) crushed pineapple
 2 tablespoons sliced pimiento-stuffed
   olives
 ¼ cup chopped cashews

 ¼ cup flour
 1 teaspoon instant chicken bouillon
   granules
 ¼ teaspoon paprika

Suggested Foods to Complete Menu:
  Carrot sticks
  Apple wedges

Preparation Sequence:
 1. Combine ingredients for chicken salad
    and chill.
 2. Prepare Swiss Cheese Soup.
 3. Cut carrot sticks and apple wedges.
 4. Assemble Chicken Salad in
    Croissants.

CHICKEN SALAD IN CROISSANTS

Makes 4 servings

2 cups diced cooked chicken
1 stalk celery, chopped
1 can (8¼ ounces) crushed pineapple,
   drained
2 tablespoons sliced pimiento-stuffed
   olives
½ cup mayonnaise *or* **salad dressing**
   Dash salt
   Leaf lettuce
4 croissants, split
¼ cup chopped cashews

In a medium bowl, combine chicken, celery, pineapple and olives. Add mayonnaise and salt; toss together lightly. Cover and chill. To serve, place a lettuce leaf in each croissant. Spoon chicken salad over lettuce; sprinkle with cashews.

SWISS CHEESE SOUP

Makes 4 servings

3 tablespoons butter *or* **margarine**
¼ cup flour
1 teaspoon instant chicken bouillon
   granules
¼ teaspoon paprika
3½ cups milk
6 slices processed Swiss cheese
1 teaspoon snipped chives

Melt butter in a medium saucepan. Stir in flour, bouillon granules and paprika. Cook and stir over medium heat until bubbly. Add milk all at once. Cook and stir until thick and bubbly; cook and stir 1 minute more. Stir in cheese and chives. Stir over low heat until cheese melts.

Chicken Stir-Fry, page 38.

Chicken and Mushrooms in Tarragon Sauce*
Chicken-Flavored Rice*
Broccoli with Cashews*
Bananas Suzette*

Shopping List:
- 2 whole chicken breasts, skinned and boned
- 1 package (10 ounces) frozen broccoli spears
- 1½ cups sliced fresh mushrooms
- 4 firm ripe bananas
- ½ cup orange juice
- 1 teaspoon finely shredded orange rind
- 2 teaspoons finely shredded lemon rind
- 1 cup whipping cream
- 5 tablespoons butter or margarine
- 2 tablespoons cooking oil
- ⅔ cup long-grain rice
- 1 can (10¾ ounces) condensed chicken broth
- ¼ cup coarsely chopped cashews
- 2 teaspoons flour
- 6 tablespoons sugar
- 2 tablespoons orange liqueur
- 1 tablespoon instant chopped onion
- ¼ teaspoon dried tarragon

Preparation Sequence:
1. Prepare Chicken-Flavored Rice.
2. Assemble ingredients for Bananas Suzette and set aside.
3. Cook chicken and mushrooms in oil.
4. Cook broccoli spears.
5. Prepare cashew-butter sauce.
6. Complete preparation of Chicken and Mushrooms in Tarragon Sauce.

CHICKEN AND MUSHROOMS IN TARRAGON SAUCE

Makes 4 servings

2 whole chicken breasts, skinned and boned
1½ cups sliced fresh mushrooms
2 tablespoons cooking oil
1 cup whipping cream
2 teaspoons flour
¼ teaspoon salt
¼ teaspoon crushed dried tarragon
Chicken-Flavored Rice

Cut chicken into 1-inch pieces. In a skillet, cook and stir chicken and mushrooms in hot oil over medium-high heat for 8 to 10 minutes or until tender. Drain chicken and mushrooms, discarding pan juices; keep warm. Stir together whipping cream and flour. In the same skillet, combine cream mixture, salt and tarragon. Cook and stir until thick and bubbly. Return chicken and mushrooms to skillet. Cook and stir until heated through. Serve over Chicken-Flavored Rice.

CHICKEN-FLAVORED RICE

Makes 4 servings

1 **can (10¾ ounces) condensed chicken broth**
⅔ **cup long-grain rice**
¼ **cup water**
1 **tablespoon instant chopped onion**
1 **tablespoon butter** *or* **margarine**
½ **teaspoon salt**

In a 1-quart casserole, combine broth, rice, water, onion, butter and salt. Bake, covered, at 350°, about 50 minutes or until rice is tender; stir once or twice.

BROCCOLI WITH CASHEWS

Makes 4 servings

1 **package (10 ounces) frozen broccoli spears**
¼ **cup coarsely chopped cashews**
1 **tablespoon butter** *or* **margarine**
2 **teaspoons finely shredded lemon rind**

Cook broccoli; drain. In a small skillet, cook and stir cashews in hot butter for 1 to 2 minutes or until golden brown. Remove from heat; stir in lemon rind. Pour over broccoli spears.

BANANAS SUZETTE

Makes 4 servings

3 **tablespoons butter** *or* **margarine**
1 **teaspoon finely shredded orange rind**
½ **cup orange juice**
6 **tablespoons sugar**
2 **tablespoons orange liqueur**
4 **firm ripe bananas, halved lengthwise**

In a large skillet, melt butter; stir in orange rind, orange juice and sugar. Bring to a boil; cook and stir for 4 to 5 minutes or until slightly thickened. Stir in liqueur. Add bananas; heat through, spooning sauce over bananas. Serve immediately.

Chicken Stir-Fry*
Hot Cooked Rice
Mixed Fruit with Sherbet*

Shopping List:
  2 whole chicken breasts, skinned and boned
1½ cups sliced fresh mushrooms
  2 stalks celery
  6 green onions
1½ cups bean sprouts
  2 slices gingerroot
  1 package (10 ounces) frozen mixed fruit (in quick-thaw pouch)
    Orange sherbet
  3 tablespoons cooking oil
    Rice
  ½ cup chicken broth
  3 tablespoons cornstarch

  1 teaspoon sugar
  2 tablespoons creme de banana or orange liqueur
  1 tablespoon dry white wine

Preparation Sequence:
  1. Cut chicken and marinate in cornstarch-wine mixture.
  2. Thaw fruit.
  3. Cook rice according to package directions.
  4. Combine fruit and liqueur, then chill until serving time.
  5. Complete preparation of Chicken Stir-Fry.

CHICKEN STIR-FRY

Makes 4 servings

2 whole chicken breasts, skinned and boned
3 tablespoons cornstarch
1 tablespoon dry white wine
1 teaspoon sugar
½ teaspoon salt
½ cup chicken broth
3 tablespoons cooking oil
2 slices gingerroot
1½ cups sliced fresh mushrooms
2 stalks celery, diagonally sliced
6 green onions, sliced into 1-inch lengths
1½ cups bean sprouts
Hot cooked rice

Cut chicken into 1-inch pieces. Sprinkle with 2 tablespoons of cornstarch and wine; mix well. Let stand at room temperature for 20 to 30 minutes. In a small bowl, combine remaining 1 tablespoon cornstarch, sugar and salt; stir in chicken broth. Set aside. Preheat wok or large skillet over high heat; add 2 tablespoons of oil and gingerroot. Heat until gingerroot begins to brown. Remove gingerroot and discard. Add chicken to wok; stir-fry in hot oil for 4 to 5 minutes or until tender. Remove from wok; keep warm. Heat remaining 1 tablespoon oil in wok; add mushrooms, celery and green onions. Stir-fry for 3 to 4 minutes or until tender-crisp. Return chicken to wok; stir in bean sprouts. Stir cornstarch mixture; blend into wok. Cook and stir until thick and bubbly. Cook and stir 1 to 2 minutes more. Serve with rice.

Swiss Cheese Soup, page 34.

MIXED FRUIT WITH SHERBET

Makes 4 servings

1 package (10 ounces) **frozen mixed fruit (in quick-thaw pouch), thawed**
2 tablespoons **creme de banana** *or* **orange liqueur**
   Orange sherbet

Combine fruit and liqueur; spoon into dessert dishes. Top each serving with a scoop of sherbet.

Cheesy Chicken and Noodles*
Broccoli Sauté*
Fruit and Yogurt Salad*
Melon Melba*

Shopping List:
   2 cups diced cooked chicken
   ½ of a 16-ounce package loose-pack frozen cut broccoli
   1 stalk celery
   2 green onions
      Leaf lettuce
   1 teaspoon snipped parsley
   2 medium apples
   1 cup seedless green grapes
   3 cups cubed honeydew melon
   1 package (10 ounces) frozen raspberries (in quick-thaw pouch)
   ½ cup sour cream
   ½ cup strawberry yogurt
   ½ of an 8-ounce jar cheese spread
   2 tablespoons butter or margarine
   6 ounces medium noodles
   ½ cup mandarin orange sections
   ¼ cup flaked coconut
   1 tablespoon flour
   2 tablespoons plus ½ teaspoon sugar
   1 teaspoon cornstarch
   2 teaspoons instant chicken bouillon granules

Preparation Sequence:
   1. Thaw fruit.
   2. Cook noodles.
   3. Prepare Fruit and Yogurt Salad.
   4. Prepare sauce for Melon Melba.
   5. Start Broccoli Sauté.
   6. Complete preparation of Cheesy Chicken and Noodles.

CHEESY CHICKEN AND NOODLES

Makes 4 servings

3 cups **water**
2 teaspoons **instant chicken bouillon granules**
½ teaspoon **salt**
6 ounces **medium noodles**
½ cup **sour cream**
1 tablespoon **flour**
2 cups **diced cooked chicken**
½ of an 8-ounce jar **cheese spread**
1 teaspoon **snipped parsley**

In a medium saucepan, bring water, bouillon granules and salt to a boil; stir in noodles. Return to a boil; reduce heat and simmer, uncovered, for 10 minutes, stirring occasionally. In a bowl, stir together sour cream and flour. Stir chicken, cheese spread, parsley and sour cream mixture into undrained noodles. Cook and stir until thick and bubbly. Cook and stir 1 minute more.

BROCCOLI SAUTÉ

Makes 4 servings

½ **of a 16-ounce package loose-pack frozen cut broccoli**
1 **stalk celery, sliced**
2 **green onions, sliced**
2 **tablespoons butter** or **margarine**
½ **teaspoon sugar**
¼ **teaspoon salt**

In a large skillet, cook and stir broccoli, celery and green onion in hot butter over medium-high heat about 8 minutes or until tender-crisp. Stir in sugar and salt.

FRUIT AND YOGURT SALAD

Makes 4 servings

Leaf lettuce
2 **medium apples, chopped**
1 **cup seedless green grapes, halved**
½ **cup mandarin orange sections**
¼ **cup flaked coconut**
½ **cup strawberry yogurt**

Line individual salad plates with leaf lettuce. Combine apples, grapes, mandarin oranges and flaked coconut; toss lightly. Spoon fruit mixture onto lettuce-lined plates. Drizzle strawberry yogurt over fruit.

MELON MELBA

Makes 4 servings

1 **package (10 ounces) frozen raspberries (in quick-thaw pouch), thawed**
1 **to 2 tablespoons sugar**
1 **teaspoon cornstarch**
3 **cups cubed honeydew melon**

Drain raspberries; reserve juice. In a small saucepan, combine sugar and cornstarch; stir in reserved juice. Cook and stir over medium heat until thick and bubbly; cook and stir for 2 minutes more. Remove from heat; stir in berries. Cool. To serve, spoon melon into dessert dishes; top with berry sauce.

Chicken Livers in Patty Shells*
Sautéed Carrots and Onions*
Fresh Greens   Tarragon-Oil Dressing*
Fresh Peach Compote*

Shopping List:
12 ounces chicken livers
2 slices bacon
1 pound carrots
1 medium onion
1½ cups sliced fresh mushrooms
3 medium peaches
2 tablespoons lemon juice
2 tablespoons frozen lemonade
    concentrate
4 frozen patty shells
⅓ cup milk
1 package (3 ounces) cream
    cheese
2 tablespoons butter or margarine
½ cup olive or salad oil
3 tablespoons tarragon vinegar
2 tablespoons light corn syrup
2 tablespoons orange liqueur
1 teaspoon flour

½ teaspoon sugar
1 teaspoon Dijon-style mustard
1 teaspoon Worcestershire sauce
1 clove garlic
1 teaspoon snipped chives

Suggested Foods to Complete Menu:
Fresh greens

Preparation Sequence:
1. Bake frozen patty shells.
2. Prepare Tarragon-Oil Dressing
   and chill.
3. Prepare Fresh Peach Compote and
   chill.
4. Fry bacon.
5. Start cooking Sautéed Carrots and
   Onions.
6. Prepare Chicken Livers in Patty
   Shells.
7. Toss fresh greens with dressing.

CHICKEN LIVERS IN PATTY SHELLS

Makes 4 servings

4 frozen patty shells
2 slices bacon
12 ounces chicken livers, coarsely
    chopped
1½ cups sliced fresh mushrooms
⅓ cup milk
1 teaspoon flour
1 package (3 ounces) cream cheese,
    cubed
1 teaspoon snipped chives
1 teaspoon Worcestershire sauce
½ teaspoon salt

Bake patty shells. In a skillet, fry bacon until crisp. Remove bacon and drain, reserving drippings in the skillet. Crumble bacon and set aside. In reserved drippings, cook chicken livers and mushrooms over medium-high heat for 6 to 8 minutes or until tender. Remove from skillet, reserving pan juices; keep warm. Blend milk and flour. In the same skillet, combine reserved pan juices, milk mixture, cream cheese, chives, Worcestershire and salt. Cook and stir until thick and bubbly. Add livers and mushrooms; cook and stir until heated through. Spoon into patty shells; sprinkle with reserved bacon.

Chicken Salad in Croissants, page 34.

SAUTÉED CARROTS AND ONIONS

Makes 4 servings

1 pound carrots, cut into julienne strips
1 medium onion, sliced
2 tablespoons butter *or* margarine
½ teaspoon sugar
¼ teaspoon salt

In a skillet, cook carrots and onion in hot butter over medium-high heat for 8 to 10 minutes or until tender-crisp, stirring frequently. Stir in sugar and salt.

TARRAGON-OIL DRESSING

Makes about ¾ cup

½ cup olive *or* salad oil
3 tablespoons tarragon vinegar
2 tablespoons lemon juice
1 teaspoon Dijon-style mustard
1 clove garlic, minced
⅛ teaspoon salt
   Dash pepper
   Fresh greens

In a screw-top jar, combine oil, vinegar, lemon juice, mustard, garlic, salt and pepper. Cover and shake thoroughly. Chill. Shake again before serving over fresh greens.

FRESH PEACH COMPOTE

Makes 4 servings

2 tablespoons light corn syrup
2 tablespoons frozen lemonade
   concentrate, thawed
2 tablespoons orange liqueur
3 medium peaches

Combine corn syrup, lemonade concentrate and liqueur; set aside. Peel, pit and slice peaches. Pour syrup mixture over peaches; stir thoroughly to coat. Cover and chill. Stir again before serving.

Menus with Fish

Halibut with Mushrooms*
Saffron Rice*
Cucumber-Pea Salad*
Strawberries with Cream*

Shopping List:
1 pound fresh *or* frozen halibut *or* other fish steaks, cut 1 inch thick
1½ cups sliced fresh mushrooms
3 cups torn lettuce
1 small cucumber
1 cup frozen peas
2 tablespoons snipped parsley
2 cups fresh strawberries
1 lemon
¼ cup sour cream
¼ cup whipping cream
¼ cup butter *or* margarine
⅓ cup salad oil
½ of a 4-ounce container frozen whipped dessert topping
⅔ cup long-grain rice
½ of a 3-ounce can French-fried onions
2 tablespoons plus 1 teaspoon sugar

2 tablespoons vinegar
¼ teaspoon dry mustard
¼ teaspoon paprika
¼ teaspoon dried dillweed
¼ teaspoon dried tarragon
⅛ teaspoon saffron
⅛ teaspoon cinnamon
Seasoning salt

Preparation Sequence:
1. Prepare Saffron Rice.
2. Combine strawberries and sugar, then chill.
3. Prepare topping mixture for Strawberries with Cream.
4. Start preparation of Cucumber-Pea Salad.
5. Prepare Halibut with Mushrooms.
6. Toss salad with dressing.

HALIBUT WITH MUSHROOMS

Makes 4 servings

1 pound fresh *or* frozen halibut, thawed *or* other fish steaks, cut 1 inch thick
1 tablespoon butter *or* margarine, melted
Seasoning salt
1½ cups sliced fresh mushrooms
1 tablespoon butter *or* margarine
¼ cup whipping cream
¼ teaspoon dried dillweed
Lemon wedges

Rinse fish and pat dry. Arrange in a 12 x 7½ x 2-inch baking dish. Brush with melted butter, then sprinkle with seasoning salt. Bake, uncovered, at 450° for 8 to 12 minutes or until fish flakes easily when tested with a fork. In a skillet, sauté mushrooms in 1 tablespoon hot butter over medium-high heat for 3 minutes. Stir in cream and dillweed. Bring to a boil. Reduce heat and simmer, uncovered, for 3 to 4 minutes or until slightly thickened. Serve over fish; garnish with lemon wedges.

SAFFRON RICE

Makes 4 servings

1⅓ **cups cold water**
⅔ **cup long-grain rice**
2 **tablespoons butter** *or* **margarine**
¾ **teaspoon salt**
⅛ **teaspoon saffron**
2 **tablespoons snipped parsley**

In a saucepan, combine water, rice, butter, salt and saffron. Cover and bring to a boil. Reduce heat. Simmer, covered, for 15 minutes. Remove from heat. Let stand, covered, for 10 minutes. Stir in parsley.

CUCUMBER-PEA SALAD

Makes 4 servings

1 **cup frozen peas**
⅓ **cup salad oil**
2 **tablespoons vinegar**
1 **teaspoon sugar**
¼ **teaspoon dry mustard**
¼ **teaspoon paprika**
¼ **teaspoon dried tarragon, crushed**
3 **cups torn lettuce**
1 **small cucumber, peeled and chopped**
½ **of a 3-ounce can French-fried onions, coarsely crushed**

Pour boiling water over frozen peas; let stand for 2 minutes. Drain thoroughly. For dressing, in a screw-top jar, combine oil, vinegar, sugar, dry mustard, paprika and tarragon. Cover and shake thoroughly. In a salad bowl, combine lettuce, cucumber and peas; toss with dressing. Sprinkle with French-fried onions.

STRAWBERRIES WITH CREAM

Makes 4 servings

2 **cups fresh strawberries, quartered**
2 **tablespoons sugar**
½ **of a 4-ounce container frozen whipped dessert topping, thawed**
¼ **cup sour cream**
⅛ **teaspoon cinnamon**

Sprinkle strawberries with 1 tablespoon of sugar; cover and chill. In a bowl, combine dessert topping, sour cream, cinnamon and remaining sugar. To serve, spoon strawberries into dessert dishes; top with cream mixture.

Halibut with Mushrooms, page 45;
Cucumber-Pea Salad, page 47.

Broiled Shrimp Kebabs*
Pasta and Pea Pods*
Bananas with Rum Cream*

Shopping List:

1 pound fresh *or* frozen large shrimp in shells
1 package (6 ounces) frozen pea pods
1 carrot, optional
4 small bananas
4 lemon slices
1 egg
¼ cup grated Romano cheese
½ cup butter *or* margarine
¼ cup cooking oil
½ of a 4-ounce container frozen whipped dessert topping
8 ounces mostaccioli
¼ cup brown sugar
1 tablespoon dark rum
Chocolate curls, optional
4 whole allspice
3 garlic cloves
1 teaspoon dried tarragon
1 teaspoon dried oregano
Bay leaves, optional

Preparation Sequence:

1. Peel and devein shrimp.
2. Combine ingredients for marinade; add shrimp.
3. Prepare Rum Cream.
4. Cook mostaccioli and pea pods.
5. Thread shrimp on skewers and broil.
6. Complete preparation of Pasta and Pea Pods.

PASTA AND PEA PODS

Makes 4 servings

8 ounces mostaccioli
1 package (6 ounces) frozen pea pods, cooked
½ cup butter *or* **margarine**
Salt
Pepper
¼ cup grated Romano cheese
Julienned carrots, optional

Cook mostaccioli and pea pods; drain and keep warm. In a skillet, melt butter over medium heat until golden brown. Remove from heat; add mostaccioli and pea pods. Toss together. Season to taste with salt and pepper. Transfer to a serving bowl; sprinkle with Romano. Garnish with julienned carrots, if desired.

BANANAS WITH RUM CREAM

Makes 4 servings

1 egg, separated
¼ cup brown sugar
1 tablespoon dark rum
½ of a 4-ounce container frozen whipped dessert topping, thawed
4 small bananas, sliced
Chocolate curls, optional

In a small mixer bowl, beat egg white until soft peaks form; gradually add half of the brown sugar, beating until stiff peaks form. Transfer to a clean bowl. In the same mixer bowl, beat egg yolk until thick and lemon colored; beat in remaining brown sugar and rum. Fold egg white and dessert topping into yolk mixture. Chill until serving time. To serve, place sliced bananas in 4 dessert dishes. Spoon rum cream over fruit. Garnish with chocolate curls, if desired.

BROILED SHRIMP KEBABS

Makes 4 servings

1 **pound fresh** or **frozen large shrimp
   in shells, thawed**
¼ **cup cooking oil**
4 **lemon slices**
4 **whole allspice**
3 **garlic cloves, minced**
1 **teaspoon crushed dried tarragon**
1 **teaspoon crushed dried oregano
   Bay leaves, optional**

Peel and devein shrimp, leaving the tail intact, if desired. In a shallow dish, combine oil, lemon, allspice, garlic, tarragon and oregano. Add shrimp. Cover and marinate for 1 hour at room temperature, stirring occasionally. (Or, marinate overnight in the refrigerator.) Preheat broiler. Drain shrimp, reserving marinade; discard lemon and allspice. Thread shrimp on short skewers alternately with bay leaves, if desired. Place on unheated rack of broiler pan. Broil 4 inches from heat for 3 to 4 minutes or until shrimp turn pink; turn and brush occasionally with reserved marinade.

Oven-Fried Fish*   Tartar Sauce*
Corn on the Cob
Peas with Celery*
Coleslaw*
Watermelon

Shopping List:
   1 pound fresh or frozen perch or other
     fish fillets
   1 package (10 ounces) frozen peas
   2 cups shredded cabbage
   ½ cup sliced celery
   ¼ cup shredded carrot
   ¼ cup finely chopped onion
   1 lemon
   1 egg
   ⅓ cup sour cream
   2 tablespoons milk
   ½ cup butter or margarine
   ¾ cup mayonnaise or salad
     dressing
   3 tablespoons pickle relish
   ¼ cup fine dry seasoned bread
     crumbs

   2 tablespoons flour
   2 tablespoons sugar
   2 tablespoons vinegar
   ¼ teaspoon seasoned salt
   ¼ teaspoon dried thyme
     Garlic powder

Suggested Foods to Complete Menu:
   Corn on the cob
   Watermelon

Preparation Sequence:
   1. Prepare Coleslaw and chill.
   2. Prepare Tartar Sauce and chill.
   3. Coat fish with egg and crumb
      mixture.
   4. Cook corn.
   5. Prepare Peas with Celery.
   6. Bake fish.

OVEN-FRIED FISH

Makes 4 servings

1 pound fresh or frozen perch or other
  fish fillets, thawed, cut ½ inch thick
1 beaten egg
2 tablespoons milk
¼ cup fine dry seasoned bread crumbs
2 tablespoons yellow cornmeal
2 tablespoons flour
¼ teaspoon seasoned salt
6 tablespoons butter or margarine,
  melted
  Lemon wedges

Rinse fish and pat dry. In a shallow dish, combine egg and milk. In a second shallow dish, combine crumbs, cornmeal, flour and salt. Dip fish in egg mixture, then in crumb mixture. Place in a shallow baking pan. Drizzle fish with melted butter. Bake at 500° for 4 to 6 minutes or until fish flakes easily when tested with a fork. Serve with lemon wedges.

TARTAR SAUCE

Makes about 1 cup

¾ cup mayonnaise or salad dressing
3 tablespoons finely chopped onion
3 tablespoons pickle relish

Combine mayonnaise, onion and pickle relish; cover and chill until serving time.

PEAS WITH CELERY

Makes 4 servings

1 package (10 ounces) frozen peas
½ cup sliced celery
2 tablespoons butter or margarine
¼ teaspoon crushed dried thyme

Cook peas; drain. In a small saucepan, cook and stir celery in hot butter over medium-high heat for 3 to 4 minutes or until tender-crisp; stir in thyme. Pour over peas and toss.

COLESLAW

Makes 4 servings

2 cups shredded cabbage
¼ cup shredded carrot
1 tablespoon finely chopped onion
⅓ cup dairy sour cream
2 tablespoons sugar
2 tablespoons vinegar
⅛ teaspoon salt
  Dash garlic powder

In a bowl, combine cabbage, carrot and onion; set aside. To make dressing, in a screw-top jar, combine sour cream, sugar, vinegar, salt and garlic powder; shake until sugar dissolves. Pour over cabbage mixture; toss. Cover and chill. Toss again before serving.

Broiled Shrimp Kebabs, page 49;
Pasta and Pea Pods, Bananas with
Rum Cream, page 48.

Broiled Salmon Steaks*
Oven Potatoes with Dill*
Green Beans Amandine*
Peach Cobbler*

Shopping List:
1 pound fresh *or* frozen salmon steaks, cut 1 inch thick
1 pound new potatoes
1 package (9 ounces) frozen whole green beans
1 tablespoon plus 2 teaspoons lemon juice
1 tablespoon milk
6 tablespoons plus 1 teaspoon butter *or* margarine
1 teaspoon cooking oil
1 can (16 ounces) sliced peaches
½ cup biscuit mix
5 tablespoons sugar
2 teaspoons cornstarch
¼ cup slivered almonds
1 teaspoon Worcestershire sauce
½ teaspoon dried dillweed
½ teaspoon cinnamon

Preparation Sequence:
1. Prepare Oven Potatoes with Dill.
2. Prepare Peach Cobbler.
3. Start preparation of Green Beans Amandine.
4. Prepare broiled Salmon Steaks.
5. Combine green beans and almond-butter.

BROILED SALMON STEAKS

Makes 4 servings

1 pound fresh *or* frozen salmon steaks, thawed, cut 1 inch thick
2 tablespoons butter *or* margarine, melted
1 tablespoon lemon juice
1 teaspoon Worcestershire sauce

Rinse fish and pat dry. Preheat broiler. Combine melted butter, lemon juice and Worcestershire in a small bowl. Arrange fish on the unheated rack of broiler pan. Brush lightly with butter mixture. Broil 4 inches from heat for 5 minutes. Turn; brush again. Broil for 4 to 6 minutes more or until fish flakes easily when tested with a fork. Brush with remaining butter mixture before serving.

OVEN POTATOES WITH DILL

Makes 4 servings

1 pound new potatoes, unpeeled
3 tablespoons butter *or* margarine
½ teaspoon salt
½ teaspoon dried dillweed

Cut potatoes into quarters. Place in a 1½-quart casserole with butter, salt and dillweed. Bake, covered, at 425° for about 45 minutes or until tender, stirring occasionally.

GREEN BEANS AMANDINE

Makes 4 servings

1 package (9 ounces) frozen whole green beans
¼ cup slivered almonds
1 tablespoon butter *or* margarine

Cook beans; drain. In a small skillet, sauté almonds in hot butter for 1 to 2 minutes or until golden brown. Pour almonds over beans and toss.

PEACH COBBLER

Makes 4 servings

½ cup biscuit mix
1 tablespoon sugar
1 tablespoon milk
1 teaspoon cooking oil
1 teaspoon butter *or* margarine, softened
1 tablespoon sugar
½ teaspoon cinnamon
1 can (16 ounces) sliced peaches
3 tablespoons sugar
2 teaspoons cornstarch
2 teaspoons lemon juice

Stir together biscuit mix and 1 tablespoon sugar. Add milk and cooking oil; mix well. On a floured surface, pat biscuit dough to a 6 x 4-inch rectangle. Spread with butter, then sprinkle with 1 tablespoon sugar and cinnamon. Roll up jelly-roll style, starting at the narrow side. Cut into fourths.

Drain peaches, reserving syrup. Add water to syrup to make 1 cup. In a saucepan, combine 3 tablespoons sugar and cornstarch. Stir in syrup mixture. Cook and stir over medium heat until thick and bubbly. Stir in peaches and lemon juice; return to boiling.

Divide peach mixture among four 1-cup baking dishes. Top each with a biscuit. Bake at 425° about 15 minutes or until biscuits are golden.

Clam Chowder*
Crisp Relishes   Avocado Dip*
Pound Cake   Fresh Sliced Strawberries

Shopping List:
1 can (6½ ounces) minced clams
2 slices bacon
3 cups frozen hash brown potatoes
with onion and peppers
1 avocado
1 teaspoon lemon juice
2 cups light cream
1 cup plus 2 tablespoons milk
⅓ cup sour cream
2 tablespoons Italian salad
dressing

2 tablespoons flour
Garlic salt

Suggested Foods to Complete Menu:
Crisp relishes
Pound cake
Fresh sliced strawberries

Preparation Sequence:
1. Start Clam Chowder.
2. Prepare relishes and strawberries.
3. Prepare Avocado Dip.
4. Complete preparation of chowder.

CLAM CHOWDER

Makes 4 servings

1 can (6½ ounces) minced clams
2 slices bacon
3 cups frozen hash brown potatoes with onion and peppers
2 cups light cream
1 cup milk
¾ teaspoon garlic salt
Dash pepper
2 tablespoons flour

Drain clams, reserving juice. Add water to reserved juice to equal 1 cup; set aside. In a medium saucepan, fry bacon until crisp; drain and crumble. Set aside. Discard bacon drippings. In the same saucepan, combine hash browns and reserved clam juice mixture. Bring to a boil. Reduce heat and simmer, covered, about 8 minutes or until vegetables are tender. Stir in clams, light cream, ¾ cup of milk, salt and pepper. Blend remaining ¼ cup milk and flour; stir into clam mixture. Cook and stir over medium heat until thick and bubbly. Cook and stir for 1 minute more.

AVOCADO DIP

Makes about 1 cup

1 avocado, peeled and seeded
⅓ cup sour cream
2 tablespoons Italian salad dressing
1 teaspoon lemon juice
Dash garlic salt
1 to 2 tablespoons milk

In a bowl, mash avocado, using a fork. Stir in sour cream, salad dressing, lemon juice and garlic salt; add milk until of dipping consistency. Serve with crisp relishes.

Avocado Dip, page 54.

*Fried Rice with Shrimp**
*Vinaigrette Salad**
Pineapple Sherbet

Shopping List:
  1 cup cooked shrimp
  1 cup frozen peas
  1 cup sliced green onion
  1 medium green pepper
  1 small green pepper
  3 cups torn romaine
  8 cherry tomatoes
  1 teaspoon snipped chives
  4 eggs
  3 cups cooked rice
  ⅓ cup plus 3 tablespoons salad or
    cooking oil

  ¼ cup white wine vinegar
  4 teaspoons sugar
  ½ teaspoon dry mustard
  ½ teaspoon dried basil

Suggested Foods to Complete Menu:
  Pineapple sherbet

Preparation Sequence:
  1. Prepare dressing for Vinaigrette
     Salad.
  2. Combine salad ingredients.
  3. Prepare Fried Rice with Shrimp.
  4. Toss dressing with salad.

FRIED RICE WITH SHRIMP

Makes 4 servings

3 tablespoons cooking oil
4 eggs, beaten
1 cup sliced green onion
1 medium green pepper, chopped
3 cups cooked rice
1 cup cooked shrimp, halved
1 cup frozen peas, thawed
2 teaspoons sugar
½ teaspoon salt

In a large skillet, heat 1 tablespoon of oil; add eggs. Cook over medium-low heat until set, without stirring; top should still be soft. Slip "egg sheet" onto a plate; cut into short narrow strips. Set aside. In the same skillet, cook and stir green onion and green pepper in the remaining 2 tablespoons oil over medium-high heat for 3 to 4 minutes or until tender-crisp. Add rice, shrimp, peas, sugar and salt; cook and stir for 3 minutes. Add egg strips; cook and stir until heated through.

VINAIGRETTE SALAD

Makes 4 servings

⅓ cup salad oil
¼ cup white wine vinegar
2 teaspoons sugar
1 teaspoon snipped chives
½ teaspoon dry mustard
½ teaspoon crushed dried basil
3 cups torn romaine
8 cherry tomatoes, halved
1 small green pepper, coarsely chopped

To make dressing, in a screw-top jar, combine oil, vinegar, sugar, chives, dry mustard and basil; cover and shake thoroughly. In a salad bowl, combine romaine, tomatoes and green pepper. Shake dressing again; pour over salad and toss.

Menus for Brunch

German Oven Pancake*
Brown-and-Serve Sausage Links
Sautéed Apples*
Honeydew Melon with Lime Wedges

Shopping List:
   4 medium apples
   6 eggs
   1 cup milk
   6 tablespoons butter *or* margarine
      Melted butter *or* margarine
   1 cup flour
   2 tablespoons sugar
      Sifted powdered sugar
      Cinnamon

Suggested Foods to Complete Menu:
   Brown-and-Serve sausage links
   Honeydew melon
   Lime wedges

Preparation Sequence:
   1. Cut honeydew melon and lime.
   2. Prepare German Oven Pancake.
   3. Prepare Sautéed Apples.
   4. Brown sausage links.

GERMAN OVEN PANCAKE

Makes 4 servings

6 eggs
1 cup milk
¼ cup butter *or* **margarine, melted**
1 cup flour
¾ teaspoon salt
   Melted butter *or* **margarine**
   Sifted powdered sugar

In a blender, combine eggs, milk and melted butter. Cover and blend on low speed until mixed. Add flour and salt; cover and blend on medium speed until smooth. Pour into well-greased 13 x 9 x 2-inch baking dish. Bake at 450° for 20 to 22 minutes or until puffed and golden brown. Drizzle with melted butter and sprinkle with powdered sugar. Serve immediately.

SAUTÉED APPLES

Makes 4 servings

4 medium apples, sliced
2 tablespoons butter *or* **margarine**
2 tablespoons sugar
   Dash cinnamon

In a skillet, cook and stir apples in hot butter over medium-high heat for 6 to 8 minutes or until tender. Stir in sugar and cinnamon. Serve hot.

Tuna-Shoestring Salad*
Cherry Tomatoes
Sweet Pickles
Peach Sundae Crunch*

Shopping List:
 1 can (9¼ ounces) tuna
 2 stalks celery
 2 carrots
 ½ small onion
   Lettuce leaves
 1 teaspoon lemon juice
   Vanilla ice cream
 2 tablespoons butter *or* margarine
 ¾ cup mayonnaise *or* salad dressing
 1 can (16 ounces) peach slices
 1½ cups shoestring potatoes
 8 pitted ripe olives
 ¼ cup quick-cooking rolled oats

 ¼ cup brown sugar
 1 teaspoon prepared mustard
 ¼ teaspoon cinnamon

Suggested Foods to Complete Menu:
 Cherry tomatoes
 Sweet pickles

Preparation Sequence:
 1. Combine ingredients for Tuna-Shoestring Salad and chill.
 2. Prepare crunch mixture for Peach Sundae Crunch.
 3. Just before serving, toss tuna salad with shoestring potatoes.

TUNA-SHOESTRING SALAD

Makes 4 servings

1 can (9¼ ounces) tuna
2 stalks celery, chopped
2 carrots, shredded
½ small onion, chopped
8 pitted ripe olives, sliced
¾ cup mayonnaise *or* **salad dressing**
1 teaspoon lemon juice
1 teaspoon prepared mustard
1½ cups shoestring potatoes
   Lettuce leaves

Drain tuna; break into chunks. In a medium bowl, combine tuna, celery, carrots, onion and olives; set aside. To make dressing, combine mayonnaise, lemon juice and mustard. Add to tuna mixture; toss. Cover and chill. Just before serving, add shoestring potatoes. Toss together. Serve on lettuce leaves.

PEACH SUNDAE CRUNCH

Makes 4 servings

¼ cup quick-cooking rolled oats
¼ cup brown sugar
2 tablespoons butter *or* **margarine, melted**
¼ teaspoon cinnamon
1 can (16 ounces) peach slices, chilled
   Vanilla ice cream

In a shallow baking pan, combine oats, brown sugar, butter and cinnamon; spread mixture evenly over the bottom of the pan. Bake at 350° for 10 minutes. Remove from the oven; stir occasionally to break into small pieces as crumb mixture cools. To serve, spoon peaches into dessert dishes; top with a scoop of ice cream. Sprinkle with crumb mixture.

Spinach-Bacon Toss, page 61.

Canadian Bacon-Asparagus Stack-Ups*
Carrot Sticks
Ambrosia-Nut Dessert*

Shopping List:
8 slices Canadian-style bacon
1 package (10 ounces) frozen asparagus spears
1 cup fresh pineapple chunks
1 cup seedless green grapes
½ cup fresh blueberries
2 eggs
1⅔ cups milk
¼ cup butter *or* margarine
4 English muffins
2 tablespoons shredded coconut
1 tablespoon finely chopped pecans
2 tablespoons flour
¼ teaspoon curry powder
Paprika

Suggested Foods to Complete Menu:
Carrot sticks

Preparation Sequence:
1. Toast coconut with pecans and butter.
2. Combine fruits for Ambrosia-Nut Dessert.
3. Prepare carrot sticks.
4. Prepare Canadian Bacon-Asparagus Stack-Ups.
5. Just before serving, toss fruit with toasted coconut mixture.

CANADIAN BACON-ASPARAGUS STACK-UPS

Makes 4 servings

1 package (10 ounces) frozen asparagus spears
3 tablespoons butter *or* **margarine**
2 tablespoons flour
½ teaspoon salt
¼ teaspoon curry powder
1⅔ cups milk
2 hard-boiled eggs, chopped
8 slices Canadian-style bacon
4 English muffins, split and toasted
Paprika

Cook asparagus; drain and keep warm. In a saucepan, melt 2 tablespoons butter. Stir in flour, salt and curry. Add milk all at once. Cook and stir over medium heat until thick and bubbly; stir in eggs. Cook and stir until heated through; keep warm. In a skillet, lightly brown Canadian bacon on both sides in remaining 1 tablespoon butter. Place bacon on muffin halves; arrange asparagus over bacon. Spoon sauce over all; sprinkle with paprika.

AMBROSIA-NUT DESSERT

Makes 4 servings

2 tablespoons shredded coconut
1 tablespoon finely chopped pecans
1 tablespoon butter *or* **margarine, melted**
1 cup fresh pineapple chunks
1 cup seedless green grapes, halved
½ cup fresh blueberries

In a shallow baking pan, combine coconut, pecans and butter. Bake at 350° for 5 to 6 minutes or until lightly toasted, stirring occasionally. Cool. Combine pineapple, grapes and blueberries; add coconut mixture. Toss lightly. Spoon into dessert dishes.

Spinach-Bacon Toss*
Cheese Plate
Assorted Crackers
Almond-Fudge Bars*

Shopping List:
6 slices bacon
6 cups torn spinach
1 cup sliced fresh mushrooms
1 small onion
4 eggs
½ cup butter *or* margarine
½ cup salad oil
1⅓ cups sugar
¾ cup flour
2 squares unsweetened chocolate
½ cup semi-sweet chocolate pieces
⅓ cup chopped almonds
3 tablespoons vinegar

2 teaspoons prepared mustard
½ teaspoon celery seed
½ teaspoon almond extract

Suggested Foods to Complete Menu:
Assorted cheeses
Assorted crackers

Preparation Sequence:
1. Prepare dressing for salad and chill.
2. Prepare Almond-Fudge Bars.
3. Fry bacon.
4. Arrange cheese plate and crackers.
5. Combine salad ingredients.
6. Toss salad with dressing.

SPINACH-BACON TOSS

Makes 4 servings

½ **cup salad oil**
⅓ **cup sugar**
1 **small onion, quartered**
3 **tablespoons vinegar**
2 **teaspoons prepared mustard**
½ **teaspoon celery seed**
6 **slices bacon**
6 **cups torn spinach**
1 **cup sliced fresh mushrooms**
2 **hard-boiled eggs, chopped**

To make dressing, in a blender container, combine oil, sugar, onion, vinegar, mustard and celery seed. Cover and blend until smooth. Cover and chill. In a skillet, fry bacon until crisp; drain and crumble. In a large salad bowl, combine spinach, mushrooms, eggs and bacon; pour dressing over salad. Toss lightly.

ALMOND-FUDGE BARS

Makes 20 bars

½ **cup butter** *or* **margarine**
2 **squares unsweetened chocolate**
1 **cup sugar**
2 **eggs**
½ **teaspoon almond extract**
¾ **cup flour**
½ **cup semi-sweet chocolate pieces**
⅓ **cup chopped almonds**

In a saucepan, melt butter and unsweetened chocolate over low heat. Remove from heat and stir in sugar. Add eggs, one at a time, beating well. Stir in almond extract. Add flour; mix well. Stir in chocolate pieces and almonds. Spread in a greased 8 x 8 x 2-inch baking pan. Bake at 350° for 30 minutes. Cool; cut into squares.

Cream of Tomato Soup
Mixed Vegetable-Cheese Pie*
Vanilla Ice Cream
Chocolate-Peanut Sauce*

Shopping List:
1 package (16 ounces) loose-pack frozen mixed broccoli, carrots and cauliflower
2 cups shredded Swiss Cheese
2 eggs
¾ cup milk
2 tablespoons butter or margarine
Vanilla ice cream
1 package refrigerated crescent rolls

½ cup chunk-style peanut butter
2 squares semi-sweet chocolate
⅓ cup sugar
½ teaspoon dried dillweed

Suggested Foods to Complete Menu:
Cream of tomato soup

Preparation Sequence:
1. Prepare Mixed Vegetable-Cheese Pie.
2. Prepare Chocolate-Peanut Sauce.
3. Heat cream of tomato soup.

MIXED VEGETABLE-CHEESE PIE

Makes 6 servings

1 package (16 ounces) loose-pack frozen mixed broccoli, carrots and cauliflower
2 tablespoons butter or **margarine**
¼ teaspoon salt
¼ to ½ teaspoon dried dillweed
1 package refrigerated crescent rolls
2 beaten eggs
2 cups shredded Swiss cheese

In a large skillet, cook and stir vegetables in hot butter over medium-high heat for 6 to 8 minutes or until tender-crisp. Remove from heat; cut up larger vegetable pieces. Stir in salt and dillweed. Separate crescent rolls into 8 triangles. Place in an ungreased 10-inch pie plate, pressing over bottom and up sides to form a crust; press edges together to seal. Spoon vegetable mixture into crust; pour eggs over all. Sprinkle with cheese. Bake in a 375° oven for 20 minutes.

CHOCOLATE-PEANUT SAUCE

Makes about 1½ cups

¾ cup milk
⅓ cup sugar
2 squares semi-sweet chocolate
½ cup chunk-style peanut butter
Vanilla ice cream

In a saucepan, combine milk, sugar and chocolate. Bring to a boil, stirring constantly. Remove from heat. Using a whisk, blend in peanut butter. Stir occasionally as sauce cools. (Sauce will thicken as it cools.) Serve warm or cold over ice cream. If sauce is too thick when cold, stir in a little water.

Canadian Bacon-Asparagus Stack-Ups, page 60.

BEEF
Beef Stroganoff, 8
Beef with Peppers and Tomatoes, 6
Skillet Barbecues, 5
Steak and Onions, 11
Taco Salad, 12

BREADS
Garlic Bread, 25
German Oven Pancake, 57
Italian Toast Slices, 22
Parmesan-Parsley Rolls, 17
Seasoned Bread Sticks, 28

CHICKEN
Butter-Broiled Chicken, 32
Cheesy Chicken and Noodles, 40
Chicken and Mushrooms in Tarragon Sauce, 36
Chicken Livers in Patty Shells, 43
Chicken Salad in Croissants, 34
Chicken Stir-Fry, 38

DESSERTS
Almond-Fudge Bars, 61
Ambrosia-Nut Dessert, 60
Apple-Blueberry Crisp, 9
Bananas Suzette, 37
Bananas with Rum Cream, 48
Cherry-Oatmeal Cobbler, 22
Chocolate Cake with Broiled Icing, 17
Chocolate-Marshmallow Pudding, 28
Fresh Fruit with Marmalade Cream, 25
Fresh Peach Compote, 44
Melon in Citrus Sauce, 15
Melon Melba, 41
Mixed Fruit with Sherbet, 40

Peach Cobbler, 53
Peach Sundae Crunch, 59
Sautéed Apples, 57
Stirred Rice Pudding, 20
Strawberries with Cream, 47

DIPS AND DRESSINGS
Avocado Dip, 54
Blue Cheese Dressing, 31
Dill Dip, 5
Honey-French Dressing, 17
Tarragon-Oil Dressing, 44

FISH
Broiled Salmon Steaks, 52
Broiled Shrimp Kebabs, 49
Clam Chowder, 54
Fried Rice with Shrimp, 56
Halibut with Mushrooms, 45
Jambalaya, 16
Oven-Fried Fish, 50
Tuna-Shoestring Salad, 59

PASTA AND RICE
Chicken-Flavored Rice, 37
Mostaccioli Bake, 24
Pasta and Pea Pods, 48
Saffron Rice, 47
Spaghetti Carbonara, 27

PORK AND SAUSAGE
Barbecue-Style Pork Chops, 13
Broiled Ham with Apricot Glaze, 18
Canadian Bacon-Asparagus Stack-Ups, 60
Jambalaya, 16
Minestrone with Sausage, 21
Pork Chops with Brown Rice, 29

SALADS
Avocado-Orange Salad, 20
Boston Lettuce Salad, 6
Coleslaw, 50
Cucumber-Pea Salad, 47

Fruit and Yogurt Salad, 41
Green Salad Toss, 22
Italian Salad, 28
Mixed Green Salad, 31
Mixed Vegetable Salad, 15
Romaine and Artichoke Toss, 33
Spinach-Bacon Toss, 61
Taco Salad, 12
Tomato-Cucumber Salad, 9
Tuna-Shoestring Salad, 59
Vinaigrette Salad, 56

SAUCES
Blueberry Sauce, 33
Chocolate-Peanut Sauce, 63
Hot Butter-Pecan Sauce, 12
Tartar Sauce, 50

SOUPS
Clam Chowder, 54
Minestrone with Sausage, 21
Swiss Cheese Soup, 34

VEGETABLES
Asparagus with Sesame Seed, 9
Broccoli Sauté, 41
Broccoli with Cashews, 37
Broiled Tomatoes, 31
Cauliflower with Almond-Dill Butter, 20
Corn with Mushrooms, 33
Green Beans Amandine, 53
Hash Browns Au Gratin, 15
Hash Browns with Cheese, 11
Mixed Vegetable-Cheese Pie, 63
Oven Potatoes with Dill, 52
Peas with Celery, 50
Sautéed Carrots and Onions, 44
Seasoned Italian Green Beans, 25